NEW-GENERATION AFRICAN POETS

A CHAPBOOK BOX SET

TANO

AN INTRODUCTION IN TWO MOVEMENTS BY

KWAME DAWES & CHRIS ABANI

Published by Akashic Books
©2018 Kwame Dawes and Chris Abani

ISBN for full box set: 978-1-61775-623-8
Library of Congress Control Number for full box set: 2017956422

Akashic Books
Brooklyn, New York, USA
Ballydehob, Co. Cork, Ireland
Twitter: @AkashicBooks
Facebook: AkashicBooks
E-mail: info@akashicbooks.com
Website: www.akashicbooks.com

African Poetry Book Fund
Prairie Schooner
University of Nebraska
110 Andrews Hall
Lincoln, Nebraska 68588

For Lorna,
Sena, Kekeli, and Akua,
Mama the Great,
and the tribe: Gwyneth, Kojo, Aba, Adjoa, Kojovi.
K.D.

*

For Daphne, Michael, Mark, Charles, Greg, Stella—my family.
I love you.
C.A.

NEW-GENERATION AFRICAN POETS (TANO)

Introduction by Kwame Dawes and Chris Abani

CONTENTS OF BOX SET

NEW-GENERATION AFRICAN POETS (TANO)
Introduction in Two Movements
by Kwame Dawes and Chris Abani

PART ONE
The Wonderful Limitations of What we Know

Anyone who has been following the progress of the African
Poetry Book Fund's Chapbook Box Set Series might have
noticed that each year the number of chapbooks included in the
set has been growing. This year, we have included eleven poets
in the series. While the numbers have changed, nothing has
changed significantly in how we have approached the series. We
have continued to seek out recommendations from many people
around the world who are either poets or engaged in the busi-
ness of poetry and the literary arts; we have continued to pay
careful attention to the submissions we receive for the Sillerman
First Book Prize for African Poetry; we have continued to work
closely with the Brunel International Poetry Prize to spot prom-
ising poets who have entered that important contest; we have
continued to scour the Internet and some key places like the re-
markable Badalisha Poetry Exchange website; we have followed
blogs, news items, tweets, and Facebook in search of noise about
exciting voices; and we have come to rely on the generosity and
insight of the growing list of poets we have already published—

to find a long list of new poets who we approach and invite to submit work for consideration for the box set.

While not comprehensive, what we do is diligent and thorough. We do not give these poets a great deal of time to put together a chapbook manuscript. We are, alas, limited by the time demands of putting out such a collection each year. This year, almost fifty poets sent us manuscripts. We selected eleven. The quality of the work could justify even more poets. But there are constraints. At the same time, what has happened is that the quality of the work has become even more impressive and exciting, making the selection extremely challenging—and exhilarating.

Yet each year we are faced with some important questions, and we can't pretend to have answers to these questions. But before I even embark on this discussion, I have to say that undergirding the selections for these box sets is the very human fact of this editorial partnership. Chris Abani and I have always been happy to engage in discussions about aesthetics, quality, prosody, style, and much else, fully aware that we do not pretend *objectivity* in how we make these selections. We are also aware that we are shaped by the wide range of poetry we have read and listened to and studied over the years, poetry especially from all parts of Africa and from the African diaspora. What we have come to perceive as *taste* has derived from the wonderful and inevitable limitations of what we know. But we are also aware of the fact that we pay a great deal of attention to the ways in which the poets we are encountering are shaping poetic discourse wherever they are. We wait for the work to come, and then we let the work affect us, and from there, we begin to think of the choices that might be made.

So a quick review of the poets we see included here indicates a heavy Nigerian presence—five of the eleven poets are Nigerian (Kechi Nomu, Omotara James, Rasaq Malik, Romeo Oriogun, and Saddiq Dzokogi). Tellingly, of the five, four of them (excepting James, who lives in the US) currently reside in Nigeria, joining Alexis Teyie from Kenya, who also resides on the continent. Six of the poets collected here (Henk Rossuow, Leila Chatti, Amanda Bintu Holiday, Umniya Najaer, Yalie Kamara, and Omotara James, as mentioned above) have *dual* places of connection if not identity, and in each case they are either US-based or living in the UK. We have been interested in the question of the extent to which residency affects or shapes the work that we get, although the APBF has always worked under the assumption that access to publishing, to books of contemporary poetry, and to a community of poets that is in dialogue with each other across nation states, will impact the quality and quantity of the poetry generated by poets based in Africa. It appears to me that the bigger question the poets are tackling is how to negotiate the multiple aesthetics of region, nation, continent, and the wider world, even as they seek to have a presence in a literary world that brings its own demands to the table. We have always sought to trust that the poets, once given the resources and encouragement to generate work with the hope of having it published or shared, will work these matters out and give us the answers based on the writing they have produced. Put another way, we have sought to have an attitude of openness and genuine interest in what these poets manage to produce and what they are passionate about whenever we have opened the doors to seeing new work and selecting it.

In a recent unpublished interview, Chris Abani made the following observation in comparing the new poets with the

African poets of the past, who, he proposed, sought to find "convergences around the ideas of self":

> *What is surprising about this new group of poets is the aesthetic range. We've probably published more experimental poetry in the chapbook series than probably has ever been published by African poets writing in the English language. Which is remarkable. So we have everything from L=A=N=G=U=A=G=E poets, we have performance poets, we have standard lyric poets, we have narrative poets, we have poets who have found an orality in African epic forms and cast them with a modern sensibility, and so much more. We are seeing also that what may not normally be thought of as an aesthetic range is beginning to emerge. We have created an aesthetic safe space where poets themselves, whose sexuality might not be accepted within the context of their religions in Africa or their immediate culture in Africa, are using this opportunity to sort of emerge, to come out, not just in a sexual-identity way, but in ways in which that part of an African self can have a deep impact on the aesthetics that are needed to express it. So we see new forms emerge, new kinds of beauty emerge, new articulations of self emerge, and that in itself is a beautiful thing to watch.*

Here, he expresses something that has been quite obvious to us, and something that has made us reluctant at this stage of matters to start making broad statements about the nature of African poetry in ways that would suggest a singular aesthetic movement or discourse. What Abani points to is that the work reflects the very eclecticism that characterizes a continent, and in this multitude of voices and sounds we find a wonderful

defiance of the kind of reductionist thinking that has played
no small part in excluding African poets from many important
forums around the world. But Abani also goes on to affirm that
we, as editors, have been beneficiaries of this richness; we have
come to appreciate, through the remarkable energy and inno-
vations of these poets, that which is possible in the emerging
African poetry.

We have now arrived at our fifth box set. When this process
began, the goal that made sense to us was to produce a box set
each year for ten years. We are, therefore, halfway there now. The
logic was to think of the number of African poets who we could
see in print over a ten-year period. Already, the impact of this
project confirms one basic thing that we have always suspected:
the issue with African poetry has never been one of the absence
of talent, but the absence of access and the lack of publishing
opportunities.

—Kwame Dawes

And so here we are again, completing another African Poetry chapbook set, our fifth. Right off the bat, I think it is important to note that the term *chapbook* here is less about importance and more of scale; scale of production and number versus the economics of the moment that a small fund like ours has to contend with. But in terms of scope, quality, and excellence, these books are just that, books. Small though they may be, they are powerful collections of poems by poets of incredible, and still developing, talent, vision, and capacity.

In five years we have been fortunate to curate, publish, and usher into a global presence forty-four new African poets in this series. This is significant for a number of reasons—the volume of work over this short a time period has generated an intense interest in African poetry as a vibrant living force, contemporary in expression, and one that, while certainly political, has deep common human concerns at its center: love, a sense of self against tradition, technology, sexuality, and choice, to name but a few. It has also begun to generate an academic and research discussion once reserved only for African fiction.

The growing number of books over time also lets us chart, in a very concentrated way, the actual range and diversity not only of countries, gender, sexuality, and other sociological indices, but also of something else, perhaps even more important: that is the idea of an African poetics. Admittedly, as Kwame Dawes has so insightfully pointed out earlier in this introduction, we cannot pretend to have any definitive answers as to what this constitutes. But I think that this is what is most exciting about all of it. There is no longer a question about whether there is or can be an African poetics that is alive and always evolving, but rather the questions are now—are there multiple African poetics? Or multiple strands of one lineage? Or multiple lineages? Where do they converge and diverge? What are their particularities and overlaps? How are they developing? How much is that based on internal conversations? What are these conversations? What will happen to this ever-growing community of poets that are we are building? And so many more.

What we can state with absolute confidence is that this small intervention of ours (which is part of a number of interventions that the African Poetry Book Fund and its team of brilliant editors, and partners like the Brunel Prize, are achieving and implementing) has revealed rich seams of study, inquiry, aesthetic interventions, poetic pleasures, debates, and the sheer vibrancy of the often-ignored field of African poetry. A poetry that is not only uniquely African in concern, but transglobal in its expression and reach.

One of the most humanizing things I have had the privilege of doing is working with my friend, mentor, colleague, and brother Kwame Dawes on this chapbook project. I say *humanizing* because over the five or so years of doing this, I have read so much amazing poetry from African poets, continental and diasporic, and I realize every year how little anyone really knows about the capability of these poets—the ones we have come to know and the ones we haven't—and even after this enormous effort every year, how much more there is to know. The poems I have read have shown an exponential jump in engagement; they are personal, moving, and deeply engaged in the world.

From its nascent years, African literature has been inextricably linked to politics and the formation of the nation state. Prior to independence, the work of literature was often to create a sense of nation for West Africa (Fagunwa, Tutuola, Ekwensi, Achebe, Beti, Oyono, et al.) or for East Africa (Okot P'biet and Ngugi), and one can argue that all the books written by politicians like Awolowo and Azikiwe and Macaulay on their ideas for governance included the many movements like Negritude. This literature was driven by the need to create nationalist myths; to establish these new nations against their former colonial masters. While the modernist moments that helped define the nationhood of Europe, for instance, with individuals negotiating against the megalith monolith of state (even in protest, Orwell's *1984* is primarily about the individual human response to the state), African literature was engaged more directly with the nationalist agenda. I offer this not as a criticism of the time, or the writers of that moment, but as a way to suggest that nationalism was an imposing constraint on the way that literature could develop. The tone of the poets of that generation have the epic echo, the larger-than-life conflations, much like, say, Yeats was doing as Ireland fought for its independence. The new poets have been freed from this constraint by the generation or two before them. Now the poems are marked with a deep modernist sense of the self, as the locus for understanding culture, place, and politics. Gone are the tropes of ancestral drums, replaced with questions about the self.

I must point out here that neither Kwame nor myself are claiming to have much to do with this shift beyond the hard work of editorial curation and the intense work that has gone into creating and sustaining the African Poetry Book Fund (which is of course a group effort of the entire editorial board, the amazing publishing partners that we work with, and the generous donors like Laura Sillerman), but we are grateful to be the conduits, the agents of these new directions emerging into the world.

But I do offer this, and stand by these books, as evidence that there is a new conversation occurring in African poetry, amongst poets, between traditions and culture, between aesthetic movements and impulses, that is now available and accessible to poets, scholars, researchers, and students and fans of African literature, specifically African poetry, that wasn't there before this project emerged. This is a significant intervention, and has revealed to a larger world that poetry in Africa is as alive and as conversation-altering as fiction.

—Chris Abani

KWAME DAWES is the author of twenty-one books of poetry, most recently *City of Bones*, and numerous other books of fiction, criticism, and essays. In 2017 he coedited with Matthew Shenoda the anthology *Bearden's Odyssey: Poets Respond to the Art of Romare Bearden*. His awards include the Forward Poetry Prize, the Hollis Summers Poetry Prize, the Musgrave Silver Medal, several Pushcart Prizes, the Barnes & Noble Writers for Writers Award, an Emmy, and the Paul Engle Prize. He is Glenna Luschei Editor of *Prairie Schooner* and is Chancellor's Professor of English at the University of Nebraska. He also teaches in the Pacific Univestity MFA Program. Dawes is the artistic director of the biennial Calabash International Literary Festival, and he serves as the associate poetry editor for Peepal Tree Press and the founding director of the African Poetry Book Fund.

CHRIS ABANI's prose includes *The Secret History of Las Vegas*, *Song for Night*, *The Virgin of Flames*, *Becoming Abigail*, *GraceLand*, and *Masters of the Board*. His poetry collections are *Sanctificum*, *There Are No Names for Red*, *Feed Me the Sun*, *Hands Washing Water*, *Dog Woman*, *Daphne's Lot*, and *Kalakuta Republic*. He holds a BA in English, an MA in gender and culture, an MA in English, and a PhD in literature and creative writing. Abani is the recipient of a PEN USA Freedom to Write Award, a Prince Claus Award, a Lannan Literary Fellowship, a California Book Award, a Hurston/Wright Legacy Award, a PEN Beyond Margins Award, a PEN/Hemingway Award, and a Guggenheim Award. Born in Nigeria, he is currently Board of Trustees Professor of English at Northwestern University in Chicago.

SOKARI DOUGLAS CAMP studied fine art at the Central School of Art and Design and the Royal College of Art. Sokari has represented Britain and Nigeria in national and international exhibitions, and she has had over forty solo shows in venues such as the National Museum of African Art, the Smithsonian Institution, and the Museum of Mankind in London. Her public artwork *Battle Bus: Living Memorial for Ken Saro-Wiwa* (2006) is a monument to the writer and Niger Delta activist. In 2003, Sokari was short-listed for the Trafalgar Square Fourth Plinth contemporary art prize. In 2005, she was awarded a CBE (Commander of the Order of the British Empire) for services to art. She is an honorary Fellow of the University of the Arts London and of SOAS. *All the World Is Now Richer* will be displayed during the Venice Biennale 2017.